Pandemic, Protest, and Politics:
A LOOK BACK AT 2020

Hal Marcovitz

ReferencePoint
Press

San Diego, CA

About the Author

Hal Marcovitz is a former newspaper reporter and columnist who lives in Chalfont, Pennsylvania. He has written more than two hundred books for young readers.

Picture Credits:
Cover: Shutterstock.com

4: Shutterstock.com (upper right)
4: Shutterstock.com (lower right)
5: Shutterstock.com (upper right)
5: Shutterstock.com (middle)
5: Thomas Hengge/Shutterstock.com (lower left)
8: Alexandros Michailidis/Shutterstock.com
12: Shealah Craighead/White House/ZUMA Press/Newscom
16: Associated Press

20: MonicaNinker/iStock
22: Shutterstock.com
25: Supamotion/Shutterstock.com
29: Fiora Watts/Shutterstock.com
31: bgrocker/Shutterstock.com
35: John Rudoff/Sipa USA/Newscom
39: Stratos Brilakis/Shutterstock.com
42: ccpixx photography/Shutterstock.com
46: Yasamin Jafari Tehrani/Shutterstock.com
50: Biden Campaign/CNP/Polaris/Newscom
54: Lev_radin/Shutterstock.com

LIBRARY OF CONGRESS CATALOGING-IN-PUBLICATION DATA

Names: Marcovitz, Hal, author.
Title: Pandemic, protest, and politics: a look back at 2020 / by Hal Marcovitz.
Description: San Diego, CA : ReferencePoint Press, Inc., 2022. | Includes bibliographical references and index.
Identifiers: LCCN 2021007489 (print) | LCCN 2021007490 (ebook) | ISBN 9781678201821 (library binding) | ISBN 9781678201838 (ebook)
Subjects: LCSH: COVID-19 (Disease)--Social aspects--United States--Juvenile literature. | United States--Race relations--History--Juvenile literature. | Social problems--United States--History--Juvenile literature. | Presidents--United States--Election--2020--Juvenile literature. | Natural disasters--United States--Juvenile literature.
Classification: LCC RA644.C67 M373 2022 (print) | LCC RA644.C67 (ebook) | DDC 362.1962/414--dc23
LC record available at https://lccn.loc.gov/2021007489
LC ebook record available at https://lccn.loc.gov/2021007490

CONTENTS

IMPORTANT EVENTS OF 2020

January

- On January 16 the US House of Representatives submits two articles of impeachment to the US Senate, initiating the first impeachment trial of President Donald Trump.
- On January 30 the WHO declares a global health emergency in connection with the rapid spread of a new and deadly coronavirus.

February

- On February 5 the Senate acquits Trump on both articles of impeachment.
- On February 11 the WHO names the disease caused by the new coronavirus COVID-19 (for coronavirus disease 2019).

March

- On March 19 California becomes first US state to enact a statewide shutdown.
- On March 24 the International Olympic Committee announces a one-year postponement of the 2020 Tokyo Summer Olympics because of the COVID-19 pandemic.

April

- On April 12 a massive storm system produces more than 40 tornadoes from Texas to South Carolina, killing 32 people across 6 states.
- As of April 26, the pandemic has killed more than 200,000 and sickened more than 2.8 million people worldwide.

May

- On May 8 the US unemployment rate hits 14.7 percent — a number attributed to the massive layoffs of workers due to the COVID-19 pandemic.
- On May 25 George Floyd, a forty-six-year-old Black man, dies from a fatal chokehold applied by a White Minneapolis police officer. The incident sparks months of protests (nationwide and around the world) against racial injustice.

June

- On June 5 Joe Biden secures the Democratic nomination after winning presidential primaries held that week in seven states and Washington DC.

July

- On July 18 Oregon's attorney general sues the federal government, charging that unidentified federal agents unlawfully detained racial injustice protesters in the city of Portland.
- On July 23, after a delay of nearly four months due to the COVID-19 pandemic, Major League Baseball begins an abbreviated 60-game schedule.

August

- On August 11 Joe Biden selects California senator Kamala Harris as the Democratic Party's nominee for vice president.

- On August 27 Hurricane Laura makes landfall, slamming into several cities in Louisiana and leaving hundreds homeless.

September

- On September 9 the August Complex fire becomes the largest wildfire in recorded California history.

- On September 26 more than 200 people, most without masks, attend a White House Rose Garden ceremony for Trump's US Supreme Court nominee. Days later, Trump and other attendees test positive for coronavirus.

October

- On October 8 the FBI announces the arrests of 13 conspirators in a plot to kidnap Michigan governor Gretchen Whitmer.

November

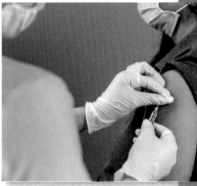

- On November 3 Democrat Joe Biden defeats President Donald Trump in the presidential election. Trump refuses to concede and alleges election fraud, sparking several weeks of unsuccessful court challenges.

- On November 16 the pharmaceutical company Moderna announces development of a vaccine for COVID-19; two days later, pharmaceutical company Pfizer also announces development of a vaccine.

December

- On December 14 the first COVID-19 vaccines are administered in the United States.

- During a December 18 meeting, Trump and his advisors discuss the possibility of imposing martial law to negate Joe Biden's victory in the presidential election. Trump's continued promotion of baseless claims of election fraud will lead to a January siege on the capitol, followed by a historic second impeachment and acquittal.

- As of December 31, the United States has documented 19.9 million coronavirus infections and more than 345,000 COVID-19 deaths—more infections and deaths than any other nation.

A Year like No Other

As 2020 came to an end, there was no shortage of people who welcomed the new year and hoped that life would improve in 2021. "2020 has been the worst year ever, for everybody,"[1] said Darnell Crittenden, who works as a security guard at a strip mall in Chicago, Illinois. Crittenden was interviewed in early August, shortly after the mall where he works was vandalized during a demonstration against racial injustice. Throughout 2020 Chicago and other cities saw widescale protests against police killings of unarmed Black men and women. Most of the protests had been peaceful, but some had turned violent.

Anger over racial injustice was just one of the many frustrations of 2020. Other events colored the year in deeply distressing hues. Early in the year the US president was impeached, tried, and acquitted on charges of attempting to enlist a foreign country to influence the 2020 election. By year's end, a pandemic had killed nearly 2 million people worldwide—with more than 345,000 of that number in the United States. A series of devastating storms and wildfires brought death and ruin to various regions of the country. And a presidential election dominated by incendiary rhetoric and swirling falsehoods brought low a democracy that was once the envy of much of the world.

There were a few bright spots in 2020: In August the World Health Organization (WHO) announced that polio had been officially eradicated on the African continent. The November US election saw the most voter participation in 120 years. And over the course of the year, global carbon emissions fell by the largest amount ever recorded. But overall it was a year of frustration, anguish, and unspeakable loss. Feelings of helplessness made all of this even worse. "Our most debilitating threat this year was a sense of helplessness, and it ran unchecked," says *Time* magazine writer Stephanie Zacharek. "Although it's universal among humans to believe in their own fortitude, Americans, in particular, are conditioned to believe they can triumph over any crisis."[2]

Ingrained in People's Memories

Most Americans felt powerless to triumph over the crises that engulfed them. The pandemic arrived quickly and infected millions of people. Tens of thousands lost friends and family members to the disease. Businesses nationwide were forced to close, leaving millions without work and income. One disaster compounded another as massive hurricanes and wildfires, fueled by climate change, destroyed whole communities. Most people who found themselves in the paths of the fires and storms had little choice but to flee. When they returned afterward, many residents of those communities found they were now homeless.

The nationwide protests over racial injustice were borne out of deep frustration with police and with inequities fostered by systemic racism. Polls showed that the protesters had widespread support from the American public. But some of the protests got out of hand. Vandalism and looting destroyed businesses caught up in this turn of events. Frustration grew among those swept up in the chaos as well as among protesters who had all along intended to make their point through peaceful protest.

Moreover, the campaign for the presidency that occurred in 2020 was often filled with incendiary rhetoric and distortions of the truth—messages that dominated the newspapers, the airwaves, and social media. Says Zacharek, "We spent countless hours stuck at home and connected to the often untrustworthy

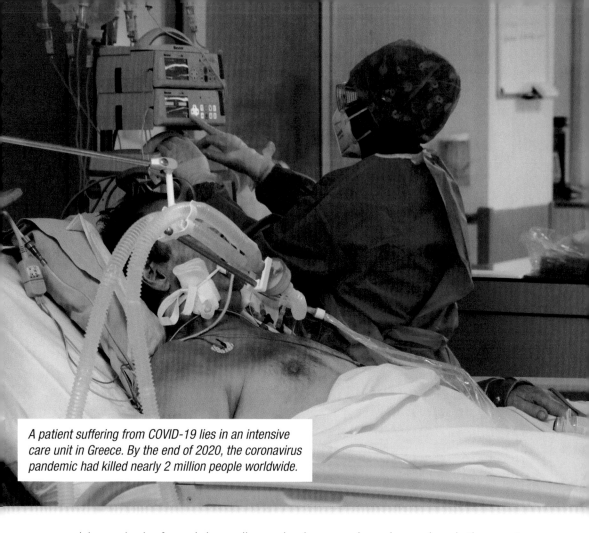

A patient suffering from COVID-19 lies in an intensive care unit in Greece. By the end of 2020, the coronavirus pandemic had killed nearly 2 million people worldwide.

hive mind of social media, wringing our hands and pointing out injustices, only to end up feeling even more paralyzed."[3]

As distressing as it was, the year 2020 is by no means the only year that has been dominated by terrible events. In 1861 eleven states seceded from the Union, touching off the Civil War. In 1918 as World War I raged, a new catastrophe arose. A Spanish flu pandemic took the lives of some 50 million people. In 1941 America was drawn into World War II when the Japanese attacked an American naval base at Pearl Harbor in Hawaii. By the time the war ended three and a half years later, more than 75 million people had lost their lives. In 1968 the Reverend Martin Luther King Jr., the nation's foremost civil rights leader, and New York senator Robert Kennedy, a candidate for president, were killed by assassins. That year was also punctuated by angry demonstrations of young people and others protesting against America's involvement in the Vietnam War.

But no one living today has a firsthand recollection of the Civil War, the Spanish flu, and other than a small number of elderly veterans and others, the attack on Pearl Harbor. And while many people alive today recall the King and Kennedy assassinations and the widespread demonstrations against the Vietnam War, most young people today know those events mostly through the pages of history books.

> "We spent countless hours stuck at home and connected to the often untrustworthy hive mind of social media, wringing our hands and pointing out injustices, only to end up feeling even more paralyzed."[3]
>
> —Stephanie Zacharek, *Time* magazine writer

But the COVID-19 pandemic, the protests over racial injustice, the wildfires and hurricanes, the impeachment of the president, and the bitter political campaign that followed are all very much a part of the lives of people in today's world. Those events will certainly remain ingrained in their memories as the world moves, hopefully, into a brighter future.

The Impeachment of President Trump

When President Donald Trump looked at early public opinion polls in June 2019, he did not like what he saw. In just seven months voters would begin casting ballots in their state caucuses and primary elections, the beginning of the process to decide who would be nominated by the two major parties for the 2020 presidential election. A Republican, Trump was not expecting competition in his party's caucuses and primaries, but on the Democratic side candidates were already lining up to seek their party's nomination. More than a dozen Democrats would soon launch their campaigns.

The polls taken at this early stage in the race showed that Trump was trailing behind several Democratic candidates. His most significant challenger promised to be Joe Biden, who spent eight years as vice president in the previous administration of President Barack Obama. On June 11, 2019, a poll conducted by Quinnipiac University in Connecticut found Trump trailing Biden by a margin of 53–40 percent. Trump realized that if Biden went on to win the Democratic nomination, Trump would be hard pressed to make up the difference, meaning he was likely to lose the presidential election in November 2020.

Elected in November 2016, Trump was a different type of leader than Americans were used to seeing hold the office of president. Dating back to the earliest days of the republic, most US presidents have come up through the country's political system. Many have served in Congress. Many have served as governors of their states. Some stepped into the presidency after serving long careers as military leaders. But Trump served no time in elective office or the military before launching his campaign for the presidency in 2015. At the time, he headed a company devoted to building hotels and apartment buildings in New York City, among other places. The world of New York real estate development can be hard fought, with competitors often resorting to underhanded ways to undermine one another. That was the culture in which Trump had thrived for decades.

As he prepared for his upcoming reelection campaign for the presidency in 2020, Trump searched for a way to attack Biden's candidacy. The action Trump is alleged to have taken would result in his impeachment in the House of Representatives and his trial in the Senate on the charge of violating the oath of office he took when he was sworn in as president.

The Call to President Zelensky

Impeachment is a process conceived by the framers of the Constitution to determine whether a US president has violated the responsibilities of his office or has broken the law. The Constitution provides for members of the House to launch an investigation and, if they find the charges have merit, to draft articles of impeachment outlining the charges. The articles then must be approved by a majority of House members. If the articles are approved, they are sent to the Senate, which stages a trial. All members of the Senate act as jurors. At the conclusion of the trial, members of the Senate vote on the guilt or innocence of the president. Two-thirds of the Senate—sixty-seven members—must vote to convict in order for the president to be removed from office.

The act for which Trump found himself facing impeachment stemmed from a phone call the president made on July 25, 2019. Shaken by the public opinion polls that showed him likely to lose the presidency the following year, Trump was desperate to find

Ukraine's president, Volodymyr Zelensky (left), meets with President Donald Trump (right) in September of 2019. In a phone conversation two months earlier, Trump had asked Zelensky to tie presidential candidate Joe Biden's son, Hunter, to a criminal investigation of a Ukrainian natural gas company.

reasons for voters to oppose Biden. He thought he had found such a reason when he learned of business dealings involving Hunter Biden, Joe's son, in the eastern European nation of Ukraine. At the time, Hunter sat on the board of Burisma, a Ukrainian natural gas company. Hunter's tenure on the Burisma board ended in 2019. But while he was still a member of the board, Burisma's president was under investigation by authorities in his own country on corruption charges.

Trump reportedly wanted to tie Hunter Biden to the Burisma president's legal problems. And so he placed a call to the president of Ukraine, Volodymyr Zelensky, asking Zelensky to launch an investigation into Hunter Biden and publicly announce that Joe Biden's son was under criminal investigation. With such an allegation hanging over the head of the son of a presidential candidate, Trump's critics say, Trump hoped to convince voters that Joe Biden had knowledge of his son's alleged corruption. As such, Trump would charge that Joe Biden was complicit in Hunter's crimes and, therefore, unqualified for the presidency.

But there was even more to the charge. Weeks after the call was made—while Trump was still waiting for Zelensky to announce an investigation of Hunter Biden—the media reported that Trump had slowed military assistance to Ukraine. At the time, the federal government was sending $400 million in weapons and other aid to Ukraine to help the nation stave off attacks along its border launched by Russia, its hostile neighbor. Critics of the president charged that Trump had slowed the military aid to pressure Zelensky into announcing the investigation into Hunter Biden.

The House Impeaches the President

Soon information about the July 25 phone call came to the attention of Congress. Under federal law, so-called whistle-blowers are able to report misconduct by officials to investigating agencies. Under law, their identities remain secret in order to protect them from retribution from those under investigation. In this case a foreign affairs analyst for the Central Intelligence Agency with knowledge of the call to Zelensky filed a whistle-blower report that was sent to members of the House and Senate.

Based on the allegations in the whistle-blower's report, the House (controlled by a Democratic majority) announced that it would pursue an investigation. The House staged a public hearing on its inquiry, which was broadcast live on national TV. The hearing, and the evidence that emerged, captivated the nation.

One of the witnesses who testified during the hearing was Alexander Vindman, a colonel in the US Army, a native of Ukraine, and a member of the White House foreign policy staff. Whenever presidents speak with foreign leaders, members of the foreign policy staff listen in on the phone calls. It is believed that following the conclusion of such calls, the staff's input in interpreting the conversations is helpful to the president. Vindman was assigned to listen in on Trump's July 25 call with Zelensky. As he listened to the call, Vindman testified during the impeachment hearing, he was shocked by what Trump asked Zelensky. "I was concerned by the call, what I heard was improper. . . . It is improper for the president of the United States to demand a foreign government investigate a US citizen and political opponent," Vindman said. "It was also clear that if Ukraine pursued an investigation into the 2016 election, the Bidens, and Burisma, it would be interpreted as a partisan play."[4]

On December 13, 2019, the House Judiciary Committee approved two articles of impeachment against the president. The first article alleged that Trump abused his power as president by placing the call to Zelensky, asking for the investigation of Hunter Biden and withholding military aid to Ukraine to pressure Zelensky to comply with his demand. The second article alleged that Trump was guilty of obstruction of justice—that during the House's investigation of the case, Trump withheld documents and other records requested by House investigators as they sought to uncover the truth.

> "It is improper for the president of the United States to demand a foreign government investigate a US citizen and political opponent."[4]
>
> —Alexander Vindman, US Army colonel and White House foreign relations adviser

Five days later the House approved the articles of impeachment by a vote of 230 to 197. All Republicans in the House voted against the impeachment of the president. On January 15, 2020, members of the House who were to serve as managers of the impeachment—essentially, the prosecutors for the trial—delivered the articles to the Senate.

The Senate Trial

On January 16, 2020, the trial commenced. In his opening remarks, Adam Schiff, a Democratic member of the House from California and one of the managers, said, "President Trump withheld hundreds of millions of dollars in military aid to a strategic partner at war with Russia to secure foreign help with his re-election, in other words, to cheat. . . . His scheme was undertaken for a simple but corrupt reason: to help him win re-election in 2020."[5]

The Impeachments of Presidents Johnson and Clinton

Prior to the impeachment of President Trump, just two US presidents had been impeached in the nation's history. In 1868 the House of Representatives voted to impeach President Andrew Johnson, alleging that he had abused the powers of his office by thwarting legislation he felt treated the southern states too harshly after they returned to the Union following the Civil War. A trial was held in the Senate, but a conviction that would have removed Johnson from office fell short by one vote.

The second impeachment occurred more than a century later. In 1998 President Bill Clinton, a Democrat, lied to federal investigators about an extramarital affair he had had with a staff member of the White House. At the time, both the House and Senate were under control of Republican majorities. Clinton was impeached in the House but acquitted in the Senate because Republicans fell short of the two-thirds majority needed to convict the president. Congressional scholars have argued that lying to cover up an extramarital affair should not be considered grounds to remove a president from office. They contend that the campaign to impeach Clinton was ginned up by Republicans purely to bring down a president from the opposition party.

For the next three weeks, the nation was captivated by the impeachment trial, which was broadcast live by several TV networks. During the trial, the president's defenders insisted the charges were contrived by Democrats who sought to bring the accusations against the president for purely political purposes. The goal, the defenders said, was to undermine Trump's standing among voters in the hopes they would turn to Joe Biden or another Democrat in the November election. Said Lindsey Graham, a Republican senator from South Carolina, "I'm not trying to pretend to be a fair juror here. What I see coming, happening today, is just partisan nonsense."[6]

The trial concluded on February 5. On the charge that Trump had abused his power, the Republican-controlled Senate

> "I'm not trying to pretend to be a fair juror here. What I see coming, happening today, is just partisan nonsense."[6]
>
> —Lindsey Graham, Republican senator from South Carolina

voted 52–48 in favor of acquittal—falling well short of the two-thirds majority needed for a conviction and to oust Trump from the presidency. The lone Republican to vote for conviction was Senator Mitt Romney of Utah, a longtime Trump critic. Said Romney, "I believe that the act [Trump] took—an effort to corrupt an election—is as destructive an attack on the oath of office and on our Constitution as I can imagine."[7] On the charge that Trump obstructed justice, the Senate voted 53–47 in favor of acquittal. On this charge, all Republican senators voted to exonerate the president.

Following the Senate's vote to acquit Trump, White House press secretary Stephanie Grisham issued a statement denouncing the campaign by Democrats to impeach the presi-

House impeachment managers address the news media in January 2020. The impeachment managers essentially serve as prosecutors during the trial in the Senate.

President Trump's critics in the Senate fell fifteen votes short of the total of sixty-seven votes needed to convict him on the impeachment charges brought by the House managers. That vote was significant for another reason: It was the first time in history that a member of the president's own party had voted to remove the president from office. Utah senator Mitt Romney, a Republican, voted to convict Trump on the abuse of power charge. During the two prior impeachments of US presidents, no members of the president's own party broke ranks to oust those presidents from office.

Trump often complained that the impeachment was spearheaded by Democrats entirely on partisan political grounds. With the exception of Romney's vote, Trump's acquittal by the Senate also followed partisan political lines. Said Republican senator Mitch McConnell of Kentucky, the majority leader of the Senate in 2020, "I'm not an impartial juror. This is a political process. There's not anything judicial about it. The House made a partisan political decision to impeach. I would anticipate we will have a largely partisan outcome in the Senate. I'm not impartial about this at all."

Quoted in Kelsey Snell, "McConnell: 'I'm Not Impartial' About Impeachment," NPR, December 17, 2019. www.npr.org.

dent. The statement said, "Today, the sham impeachment attempt concocted by Democrats ended in the full vindication and exoneration of President Donald J. Trump. As we have said all along, he is not guilty."[8]

Trump survived the impeachment effort, but he would soon learn that his path toward reelection had not been made easier by his acquittal. Four days after the Senate voted to acquit the president, a new Quinnipiac University poll showed Trump continuing to trail Biden and the other Democratic candidates in popularity among voters. For months, the nation's attention had been squarely focused on the impeachment investigation and the Senate trial—a circumstance that haunted Trump as he sought reelection in the months ahead.

"Today, the sham impeachment attempt concocted by Democrats ended in the full vindication and exoneration of President Donald J. Trump. As we have said all along, he is not guilty."[8]

—Stephanie Grisham, White House press secretary

The Pandemic

The disease first surfaced at a wet market in the city of Wuhan, China. Wet markets are common in the Asian world. They are often open-air markets where butchers slaughter livestock in front of customers buying fresh meat. Throughout Asia, wet markets are largely unregulated by governments, and stalls are rarely sanitized. In this case, many scientists have theorized that a disease carried perhaps by a bat or a pangolin caged at the wet market went zoonotic—meaning it jumped from an animal to a human. On December 31, 2019, authorities in China disclosed that dozens of Wuhan citizens were infected with severe flu-like symptoms.

A week later, the WHO, an agency of the United Nations, identified the disease as a virus, naming it COVID-19. The disease is spawned by a virus that soon overwhelms a patient's immune system. A microscopic image of the virus resembles an orb surrounded by a hazy crown. The Latin word for *crown* is "corona." Therefore, COVID-19 stands for coronavirus disease 2019. As with most viruses, it is highly contagious—able to jump from person to person in the microscopic particles contained in a person's breath. A COVID-19 patient coughing—or even just breathing—in a small room could infect many others in the room.

It did not take long for COVID-19 to reach beyond China and turn into a pandemic—a disease infecting millions of victims around the world. As physicians learned more about COVID-19, they realized it could take as long as fourteen days before patients show symptoms. In other words, for the first few days of their infection, the patients may be asymptomatic and therefore may not know they are ill. Moreover, many patients who are infected with COVID-19 never show symptoms. The disease invades their bodies, but their immune systems are able to fight it off without the patients experiencing the symptoms of high fever, severe coughing, breathing difficulties, fatigue, muscle aches, intense headaches, and loss of the senses of taste and smell. But that does not mean they cannot transmit the disease to others, who may become infected and could develop those symptoms—or worse.

Therefore, it is very likely that in the first few weeks that COVID-19 swept through Wuhan, infected but asymptomatic citizens traveled to other Chinese cities as well as foreign countries, spreading the disease to many others, who in turn continued to spread the infection. On January 20, 2020, the WHO reported cases of COVID-19 in South Korea, Thailand, and Japan. A day later, the first confirmed case of COVID-19 in America was reported. By the end of 2020, one year after the first cases were reported in Wuhan, the WHO reported the worldwide infection rate at nearly 85 million, with more than 2 million patients losing their lives to the disease. In America, 20 million people were infected with the disease, with nearly 350,000 losing their lives—a death toll of nearly 1,000 per day.

Maintaining Social Distance

Across America, nearly everyone seemed to know someone who had been infected. Most people who developed symptoms did recover, but many did not. Among the victims was Patrick McNamee, the forty-six-year-old manager of a supermarket dairy in Ypsilanti, Michigan. McNamee's mother, Annie Feeley, describes her son as a devoted father of two young children, a fan of the 1960s rock group the Beatles, and a history buff who spent many leisure hours reading books about World War II. "He was funny," says Feeley. "He was not easily angered and very easygoing."[9] In March, McNamee started showing flu-like symptoms. A few days later he drove himself to the hospital, where he spent ten days in the intensive care unit. He died on April 5.

Around the world, governmental leaders took steps to slow the infection rate by ordering strict quarantine measures to minimize the opportunities people would have to infect one another. In America, governors exercised their authority, ordering many businesses deemed nonessential to close. Among these businesses were restaurants, retail stores, movie theaters, and gyms. Many offices also closed. Employees were sent home to continue their jobs on their home computers, meeting with coworkers or customers through online videoconferencing. Schools were closed as teachers led their classes through videoconference links. People

A worker in a Chinese wet market selects eels for sale to his customers. Occasionally animals in these wet markets carry diseases that also infect humans.

were advised to maintain social distance by not coming within 6 feet (1.8 m) of one another. And when they did venture outside their homes, people were advised to wear masks over their mouths and noses that would help prevent transmission of the coronavirus. "This is a pandemic experience that's unique in the lifetime of every single person on Earth," said Sten Vermund, dean of the Yale School of Public Health in New Haven, Connecticut. "Hardly any of us haven't been touched by it."[10]

Such restrictions led to severe economic consequences for many people. Many nonessential businesses were forced to close and lay off their employees. Among those facing hardships were members of the Betancourt family in Fremont, California. Maricela Betancourt worked as a janitor, but in March 2020 the factory where she worked was forced to lay off hundreds of employees. Her husband, a construction worker, lost his job when the project where he was employed shut down. And the couple's twenty-year-old son, a college student, lost a part-time job at an arcade where he worked to help with his college costs. With no income to pay for groceries, rent, and health care costs, the Betancourts quickly went through their savings and fell deeply into debt. "As workers, we live paycheck to paycheck, and now we don't even have that paycheck, so we don't know what we're going to do,"[11] Maricela said in a May news interview.

Furor over the Lockdowns

Many people, angered at their inability to return to work or chafing under the restrictions their governors imposed on them, elected to defy orders to wear masks or maintain social distancing. They gathered for protest rallies in cities. One of the biggest rallies was staged on May 1, 2020, in Lansing, the capital of Michigan. Hundreds of protesters gathered outside Michigan's capitol building to protest restrictions Governor Gretchen Whitmer had placed on work and leisure activities in her state. The protesters demanded that restrictions be eased and all businesses allowed to reopen at full capacity. "People were just absolutely fed up with being told to stay home," protester Adam Di Angeli told a reporter. "We couldn't go to school, couldn't go to work, couldn't do anything at all."[12]

Months later, some radical antigovernment activists in Michigan took their protest a step further. On October 8, 2020, the Federal Bureau of Investigation (FBI) announced the arrests of six men, charging them in a bizarre plot to kidnap Whitmer and stage a mock trial of the governor as a protest against the COVID-19 restrictions she had ordered. Calling themselves the Wolverine Watchmen, the suspects allegedly held training sessions and were plotting to break into Whitmer's vacation home, where they planned to abduct the governor. "It was shocking," Whitmer says. "It really is something that is so personal and so serious. . . . This is happening right here in the United States of America. That's domestic terrorism."[13]

In an attempt to slow the spread of COVID-19, state governors ordered businesses like movie theaters, such as this one in Greenville, Illinois, to close.

The Shortage of Intensive Care Unit Beds

Throughout 2020 many US hospitals were so inundated with COVID-19 patients that they struggled to keep enough beds open in their intensive care units (ICUs) for all those who needed care. Patients occupying ICU beds have access to mechanical ventilators that help them breathe. They also receive care from specially trained health professionals.

December 2020 marked a low point for many US hospitals. Hospitals in El Paso, Texas, reported just thirteen beds available for new patients, down from the usual three hundred. Fargo, North Dakota, hospitals reported the availability of just three ICU beds. Hospitals in Albuquerque, New Mexico, said they had no ICU beds available.

Beth Blauer, director of the Centers for Civic Impact at Johns Hopkins University in Baltimore, Maryland, said the shortage of ICU beds affected COVID-19 patients in rural communities the most. Many had to travel miles for adequate hospital care. "There's only so much our frontline care can offer, particularly when you get to these really rural counties which are being hit hard by the pandemic right now," she said in a December news interview. "If you're living in a place where there's no ICU bed for 100 miles, you have to be incredibly careful about [your] social interaction."

Quoted in Lauren Leatherby et al., "'There's No Place for Them to Go': ICU Beds Near Capacity Across U.S.," *New York Times*, December 9, 2020. www.nytimes.com.

In Washington, Trump at times seemed to encourage anger over the COVID-19 lockdown restrictions. He was often photographed not wearing a mask. He insisted publicly the disease was not serious and that it would somehow disappear on its own. He suggested the drug hydroxychloroquine could easily cure the disease. The drug has been used for decades as a cure for the tropical disease malaria, which is spread by mosquitos. Public health experts contradicted the president, insisting that the drug would have no effect. Still, Trump continued to sympathize with the anti-lockdown demonstrators. "These are great people," Trump said. "They've got cabin fever. They want to get back. They want their life back. Their life was taken away from them."[14]

Super-Spreading Events

Since it could take as long as two weeks for a patient to show symptoms and therefore know that he or she has contracted COVID-19, it is possible for that patient to infect many others. This was particularly true in the early weeks of the disease, before some cities and states mandated that people wear masks and maintain social distancing when going out in public.

In February 2020 more than one hundred people who attended a conference for medical researchers at a hotel in Boston, Massachusetts, contracted COVID-19. Infectious disease experts who studied the outbreak concluded that a single person spread the disease at the event. Ultimately, a study published in the journal *Science* concluded that the one hundred people who were infected at the Boston conference went on to infect others, starting a chain reaction that resulted in widespread infection. The study concluded that the total number of people who contracted COVID-19 from those one hundred patients exceeded three hundred thousand. In other words, a single person who spread the virus at that Boston hotel was ultimately responsible for sickening more than three hundred thousand people. Said the authors of the study, "These estimates . . . convey the likely scope of regional, national, and international spread resulting from a single super-spreading event early in the pandemic."

Quoted in Kaitlin McKinley Becker, "Biogen Conference in Boston Now Tied to More than 300,000 Coronavirus Cases," NBC 10 Boston, December 11, 2020. www.nbcboston.com.

The Vaccines Arrive

As many citizens defied or ignored social distancing orders, great progress was made behind the scenes to develop vaccines to protect people from becoming infected. In November two pharmaceutical companies, Moderna and Pfizer, announced that they had developed vaccines for COVID-19.

Ordinarily, it takes several years for a new vaccine to be developed, tested, and approved for distribution by the US Food and Drug Administration (FDA). To develop drugs, they must be synthesized in a lab—meaning the scientists have to find the right combinations of chemicals or biological substances that make them work. Tests are often first conducted on animals. And then clinical trials are conducted with human volunteers. Clinical trials often take many months.

Meanwhile, the FDA closely monitors the trials and does not approve the drug for widespread use until the agency is satisfied that the drug is safe and effective. In the United States pharmaceutical companies typically undergo twelve years of development and trials before the FDA approves new drugs for widespread use. But after the pandemic spread across the country, the FDA approved fast-tracking measures to review the COVID-19 vaccines. On December 12, 2020, the FDA approved distribution of the Pfizer vaccine. The Moderna vaccine won approval by the federal agency on December 18. Moreover, other pharmaceutical companies made significant progress in developing their own vaccines. By February 2021, the FDA had approved a third vaccine for emergency use, this one developed by Johnson & Johnson, and others were expected to win similar approval.

Logistical Problems Slow Vaccinations
But while the world now had the means for wiping out COVID-19, logistical problems soon slowed the process. In America as well as

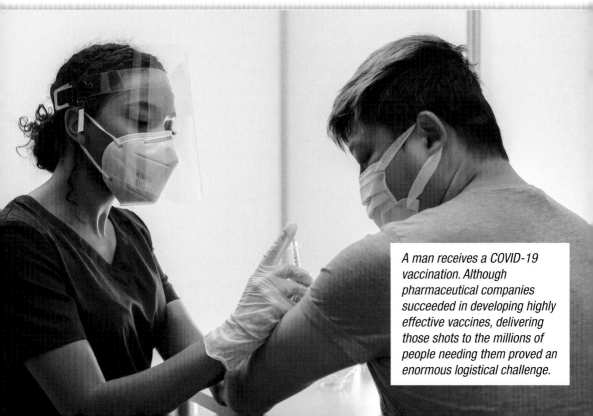

A man receives a COVID-19 vaccination. Although pharmaceutical companies succeeded in developing highly effective vaccines, delivering those shots to the millions of people needing them proved an enormous logistical challenge.

many other countries, government officials prioritized recipients for the vaccines. Health care workers—doctors, nurses, and others—were given top priority, since many of them interacted with COVID-19 patients on a daily basis. Because elderly people often have weak immune systems, meaning their natural ability to fight off the symptoms is compromised, staff and residents of nursing homes were given top priority as well. In some states other essential workers—among them police officers, supermarket employees, and delivery truck operators—were given top priority as well. In many states people age sixty-five and older were given priority for the vaccines. Soon, though, it became apparent that getting millions of doses into the arms of people was much more difficult than officials had anticipated. By early 2021, 68 million people had been vaccinated worldwide, including 23 million in the United States. But at that point, many state governments as well as foreign countries had run out of vaccine doses and were awaiting new shipments that were slow in coming.

Moreover, people who had been approved for vaccines often could not get appointments with state health agencies, retail pharmacies, hospitals, and other institutions that were authorized to provide the shots. And those who did get appointments often had to wait in line for hours, only to be told to go home because the site had run out of vaccines. In Connecticut, West Hartford resident Ethel Fried, age eighty-eight, called her state's vaccine hotline numerous times but was never able to connect with anyone to make an appointment. "It's totally frustrating," Fried said. "There's one phone line, which is nowhere near enough."[15]

By early 2021, under the administration of a new president, the federal government was trying to increase supply, while health officials were working on more effective programs to distribute the vaccine. The system to deliver health care to Americans had shown its vulnerability to a deadly disease that arrived very suddenly. That same disease had essentially caught the whole world unprepared to counter its devastating effects.

Rising Up Against Racial Injustice

For months, the COVID-19 pandemic forced American communities to remain under lockdown orders. Public health officials urged people to stay home and only go out for the most vital errands. And when people did leave their homes, they were urged to wear masks and practice social distancing. But starting in late May 2020, tens of thousands of Americans—many of them Black citizens—violated their lockdown orders to show their anger about an incident that occurred on a street in Minneapolis, Minnesota.

George Floyd, a forty-six-year-old Black man, had been arrested for allegedly using a counterfeit twenty-dollar bill to pay for a pack of cigarettes at a convenience store. In detaining Floyd, police officers wrestled him to the street. While holding Floyd down, Minneapolis police officer Derek Chauvin pressed his knee into Floyd's neck for nearly nine minutes. A witness captured the arrest on cell phone video, recording Floyd's clear distress and his last words before he lost consciousness: "Man, I can't breathe."[16]

The chokehold that Chauvin applied to Floyd's neck proved fatal. An autopsy performed on Floyd's body indicated that he lost consciousness more than a minute before Chauvin released his knee. Ambulance crew members who arrived minutes later were unable to revive Floyd; he was declared dead after being taken to a hospital.

Protests Spread to Many Cities

The video showing Chauvin press his knee into Floyd's neck was uploaded onto social media. Within hours, millions of Americans had seen it. "There are no words in the English language that will convey the despair that I felt watching that man's life leave his body," says Alicia Smith, a Black community organizer in Minneapolis. "My kids are little boys, and my son asked me, 'Am I going to live to be a grown-up?' I've got to ruin his innocence and tell him how to exist as a young black boy in this country."[17]

> "There are no words in the English language that will convey the despair that I felt watching that man's life leave his body."[17]
>
> —Alicia Smith, Black community organizer in Minneapolis

Thousands of Black protesters as well as others streamed into Minneapolis streets the following night, demanding justice for Floyd. Many clashed with police, hurling bottles and other objects at the dozens of police officers called in to quell the unrest. Police responded by tossing smoke bombs at the crowd or spraying protesters with water from fire hoses.

In the coming weeks similar scenes were repeated in numerous American cities. Two nights after Floyd's death, protests erupted in Los Angeles, California; Memphis, Tennessee; and Louisville, Kentucky. By May 30—five days after Floyd's death—protesters were streaming into the streets of dozens of American cities. "I'm really tired of seeing racial injustice across our country,"[18] says Zach Daniels, a twenty-year-old college student who participated in a protest in Chicago, Illinois.

The Birth of Black Lives Matter

For Black Americans, Floyd's death marked yet another incident in which a Black person had been abused by police. Sociologists believe racist attitudes by police toward Black citizens date back to the years following the Civil War, when former slaves, newly granted their freedom, were nevertheless targeted for abuse by police in southern states. Since those days, Black Americans have made great strides as Congress and state governments adopted antidiscrimination laws. Nevertheless, many police officers have continued to target Black citizens, often racially profiling them by assuming they are criminals simply because they are Black. And, as in Floyd's case, police have often used unnecessarily harsh and in some cases deadly force in making arrests for petty crimes.

The wave of protests that broke out in 2020 was not the first time Black Americans and others who are sympathetic to their plight have demonstrated against police misconduct. In 2014, eighteen-year-old Michael Brown was stopped on a street in Ferguson, Missouri, by a White police officer, Darren Wilson, who suspected that Brown had just shoplifted a package of cigars from a nearby convenience store. Wilson and Brown soon scuffled; Brown broke free and tried to flee. As Brown ran away from the scene, he was fatally shot by Wilson.

The incident sparked massive protests in Ferguson and other cities and helped spawn the movement known as Black Lives Matter. The national group, which helps organize protests against police injustice, was actually born the prior year when George Zimmerman, a White member of a volunteer neighborhood watch

The killing of George Floyd by a Minneapolis police officer sparked protests in dozens of American cities. Many people did not wear masks.

Protests Were Not Super-Spreaders

Months after the protests over police misconduct subsided, infectious disease experts concluded that the demonstrations were not responsible for large outbreaks of COVID-19. Although many protesters wore masks during the demonstrations, it was clear that many did not. Still, Michael Osterholm, director of the Center for Infectious Disease Research and Policy at the University of Minnesota, says studies of the protests concluded that most of the participants did not contract the disease. "We tested thousands of people," he says. "We saw no appreciable impact."

Infectious disease experts attribute the fact that the protests did not turn into super-spreader events to many factors. For starters, the protests were all outside—which experts say is the safest place to be during a pandemic because wind currents swiftly dispel germs exhaled by people, making them mostly harmless. Moreover, during the demonstrations the protesters were on the move, usually marching down city streets. Even outside, Osterholm says people in stationary crowds are more likely to become infected than people who move around a lot.

Quoted in Lawrence Wright, "The Plague Year," *New Yorker*, January 4–11, 2021, p. 49.

patrol in Sanford, Florida, was found not guilty in the shooting death of Trayvon Martin. The victim was a Black teenager who was simply walking through Zimmerman's neighborhood after buying an iced tea and a snack at a nearby convenience store. Despite the growth of Black Lives Matter and the public attention focused on the deaths of Brown and Martin, by the time Chauvin placed Floyd in a fatal chokehold, little progress had been made to erase systemic racism from the ranks of many American police departments.

Demonstrations Turn Violent

As activists flooded into the streets of American cities, some of the demonstrations went beyond peaceful protests. Some of the protests turned violent as demonstrators vandalized stores and other businesses that lined the protest routes. Cars parked along nearby streets were vandalized. Protesters broke into stores and looted merchandise from them. In other cases, protesters set fires that engulfed stores and other properties. Police responded by making hundreds of arrests.

Civil rights leaders and others insisted that the vandals and thieves were not activists dedicated to ending police misconduct but instead were troublemakers who showed up at the protests to take advantage of the chaos in the city streets. Steve Mylett, the police chief of Bellevue, Washington, witnessed what had started as a peaceful protest in his city soon go out of control. "It was a tsunami of people, and they just started running," Mylett says. "I didn't hear George Floyd's name once. I didn't hear, 'Police reform!' They just scattered throughout the city. . . . It's so unfortunate that peaceful protests got hijacked by criminal networks using them for cover. How do you ignore that this tactic was being used from coast to coast, north to south?"[19]

In many cities, officials were forced to declare curfews, preventing citizens from remaining on city streets from early evening

Some of the demonstrations for racial justice turned violent, with protesters vandalizing stores and cars parked along nearby streets.

to the following morning. In Philadelphia, Pennsylvania, Mayor James Kenney declared a curfew commencing on May 30 after many properties and vehicles were looted and vandalized in the city. "The peaceful protests earlier were touching showings of our collective grief," Kenney said of the protests in Philadelphia. "But the anger displayed now and this afternoon cannot continue."[20] In Philadelphia the curfew was lifted on June 7 after tensions eased, but city officials were forced to reinstate it from time to time as protests continued to erupt throughout the year.

Federal Agents Invade Portland

Perhaps no city saw as much violence erupt during the police misconduct protests as Portland, Oregon. Protests erupted in the city four days after Floyd's death. In other communities, local

Police Chiefs March with the Protesters

Protesters in many cities found members of police departments supporting them in their calls to end racial injustice. In some cases, police officers lining the protest routes knelt down in a show of solidarity as demonstrators marched by. In some cities, police chiefs marched alongside the protesters.

Among the police chiefs who joined the protests was Larry Boone, chief of the Norfolk, Virginia, police. On May 30, 2020, Boone marched alongside demonstrators in his city. "I want to meet with each and every one of you if we can work together," Boone told the protesters. "All policemen, folks, aren't bad." Boone also praised the protesters for remaining peaceful during the march. "You've shown the world how it's done," he said.

Another chief who joined protesters was Christopher Swanson, sheriff of Genesee County, Michigan, who marched in a demonstration in Flint Township, Michigan, on May 30. Says Swanson, "The best moment of my police career is when I said, 'Let's walk.' . . . I could feel an instantaneous peace on both sides. That would not have happened if they had not wanted to listen to what I had to say as well, so it is mutually agreed upon that I need to hear what they are saying."

Quoted in Blake Montgomery, "Police Chiefs Are Marching with Protesters Against George Floyd's Death," Daily Beast, May 30, 2020. www.thedailybeast.com.

Quoted in Meredith Spelbring, "'Let's Walk': Genesee County Sheriff Removes Riot Gear, Joins Protesters in March," Detroit (MI) Free Press, June 1, 2020. www.freep.com.

officials relied on their police departments to control the demonstrations and arrest lawbreakers, but in Portland federal law enforcement officers arrived on July 1 after several weeks of violent acts by the protesters. Among those violent acts were multiple break-ins and fires set at the Multnomah County Justice Center as well as a federal courthouse in the city.

The federal law enforcement officers were dressed in camouflage uniforms but wore no other identification indicating which agency employed them—such as the FBI, US Marshals Service, or US

> "Four or five dudes in camo jump out and start charging at us."[21]
>
> —Conner O'Shea, protester in Portland, Oregon

Customs and Border Protection. And their tactics were decidedly strong-arm. Many of the activists who were simply standing near the scenes of the protests were rounded up and taken into custody.

Conner O'Shea, a thirty-year-old Portland resident, had been attending the protests in his city nightly since they erupted after Floyd's death. He gave this account to a reporter: In the early morning hours of July 16, O'Shea and a friend were walking home after a protest when an unmarked van stopped nearby. Camouflage-wearing officers exited the van. "Four or five dudes in camo jump out and start charging at us,"[21] O'Shea says.

O'Shea and his friend ran in opposite directions. O'Shea was able to escape arrest, but his friend, Mark Pettibone, was taken into custody, where he was held for several hours in a cell, then released without being charged. "Federal agents are terrorizing the community, threatening lives, and relentlessly attacking protesters demonstrating against police brutality," the civil rights group American Civil Liberties Union said in a statement. "This is not law and order. This is lawlessness—and it must be stopped."[22]

In fact, many of the nonviolent protests were supported by city officials and others who believed it was long past time that the culture of police departments be changed. In many cities mayors marched alongside the protesters and spoke at the rallies. They were often accompanied by police chiefs who promised new procedures to root out racism in their ranks. "This is an amazing, peaceful, successful demonstration of raising the voices around freedom and justice and togetherness," said Denver mayor Michael Hancock, after joining protesters in a march in his city on June 3. "I'm proud of the demonstrations going on here tonight."[23]

Police Officers Face Justice

The protests in Denver and other cities have led officials to enact new procedures to respect the rights of Black citizens. Some city governments have opted to divert millions of dollars from the budget of their police department, using that money instead to fund social services programs that improve the lives of Black citizens in inner-city neighborhoods—thereby making it less likely that police would be called into those neighborhoods. Such initiatives often include assisting inner-city residents in finding improved housing as well as helping those with addiction problems find drug rehabilitation programs. Cities are also using the money to establish crisis response teams composed of unarmed staff members who use their negotiating skills to ease troubled tempers before situations turn violent. Such actions have been labeled "defund the police" measures.

Moreover, the police officers responsible for abusing Black citizens are themselves facing justice. In the Floyd case, Chauvin and three other police officers were fired from the Minneapolis Police Department the day after the video of Floyd's death appeared on social media.

All four officers also face criminal charges. Chauvin was charged with the murder of Floyd and faces a maximum penalty of forty years in prison if he is convicted. The three other police officers who assisted Chauvin in detaining Floyd were charged with

Some federal law enforcement officers used strong-arm tactics to quell protests in Portland, Oregon. Many of the activists who were simply standing near the scenes of the protests were rounded up and taken into custody.

aiding and abetting murder. Prosecutors allege that they stood by and did nothing as Chauvin applied his knee to Floyd's neck. If convicted, each defendant could also face a maximum penalty of forty years in prison. All the defendants in the Floyd case are expected to come to trial in 2021.

The deaths of Floyd and other victims of police misconduct touched off months of protest, chaos, and violence while Americans were already reeling from the mounting tolls of illness and death caused by the COVID-19 pandemic. Despite the dangers posed by the pandemic, the actions by thousands of protesters to defy the lockdowns and social distancing orders illustrate that many of the protesters believed they had to risk their own lives to call attention to the issue of police abuse of Black citizens.

The Fires and Storms of 2020

Brandi Stewart's career as an employee of the National Park Service eventually took her to Death Valley National Park, located in the desert along the California-Nevada border. Death Valley is one of the driest and hottest regions in America, but on August, 16, 2020, the area saw temperatures soar to 130°F (54.4°C)—a heat that Stewart says she could never imagine while growing up near Pittsburgh, Pennsylvania. "The feeling of that heat on my face, it can almost take your breath away,"[24] she says.

Climate scientists eventually determined the temperature reached in Death Valley National Park that day was the hottest temperature ever recorded on earth. In fact, in recording a temperature of 130°F that day, Death Valley broke its own record. The previous record of 129°F (53.9°C) was also set in Death Valley, on June 30, 2013, and matched in later years in the countries of Pakistan and Kuwait. "I don't think any of this is really surprising," says Jeremy Pal, a professor of environmental engineering at Loyola Marymount University in Los Angeles. "As climate continues to warm, we'd expect more of these events and more of these record-breaking temperatures."[25]

Scientists have been warning for decades about the devastating effects of climate change: the warming of the planet's surface attributed to the emissions from fossil fuels—oil, natural gas, and coal. These emissions, known as greenhouse gases, trap heat in the earth's atmosphere—just as a greenhouse captures heat from the sun to help plants grow. And these emissions have been filling the atmosphere and trapping heat since the dawn of the Industrial Revolution in the eighteenth century. This is when people started using coal to power trains and ships, gasoline to fuel their cars, and natural gas to heat their homes and cook their food.

> "As climate continues to warm, we'd expect more of these events and more of these record-breaking temperatures."[25]
>
> —Jeremy Pal, professor of environmental engineering at Loyola Marymount University

The consequences of climate change are far graver than mild winters and the occasional record-breaking temperatures recorded in places like Death Valley. Scientists believe climate change has led to more devastating storms as well as the outbreak of massive wildfires that burn through tens of thousands of acres. In 2020 there did not seem to be an end to the wildfires and storms that swept through America and other parts of the world.

Wildfires Hit the Western States

The frightening wildfires of 2020 actually began a few months earlier in Australia. By early January those fires were out of control. Some three thousand homes caught in the path of the fires had been destroyed, and twenty-eight people had lost their lives when they were trapped by the flames. Wildlife was greatly impacted as well. One of the most touching moments to emerge from the scene of the fires was a video of an Australian firefighter carrying a baby koala to safety.

Climate change contributes to the outbreak of wildfires in many ways. Higher temperatures tend to dry out plants and trees, making them more likely to act like kindling if they come into contact with sparks or flames. In places that receive snowfall, climate change often shortens winter seasons—meaning there is less snow, which causes the ground to become drier in the spring and summer. And those conditions were very much in place in America, as a mild winter ended in early 2020, making a vast number of acres in California and other states prime locations for the outbreak of wildfires.

The actual cause of a specific wildfire is often a mystery, but a 2017 study published in the journal *Proceedings of the National Academy of Sciences* found that 16 percent of wildfires are caused by lightning striking dried-out trees or patches of parched meadows, while 84 percent are caused by humans. These fires are largely not set on purpose by arsonists but could be touched off in any number of ways: sparks from a campfire igniting a branch dangling nearby or even sparks that result when a car tire suddenly goes flat. In such a case, a tire rim scraping across an asphalt road would send sparks shooting out in all directions, possibly coming into contact with dried-out brush growing alongside the road. Whatever the cause, the wind soon takes over, blowing embers onto nearby parched surfaces.

California typically experiences wildfires every year, but the state never saw as many fires as it did in 2020. In California, fires usually begin in the spring once dry conditions start settling in. The first recorded wildfire in California in 2020 erupted in Kings County in the central part of the state on May 3, burning through some 2,600 acres (1,052 ha). It was contained in four days but would soon be followed by many more fires. By the end of the year, some 9,200 separate fires erupted throughout the state, burning through 4.2 million acres (1.7 million ha). Some 10,500 homes and businesses were destroyed by the fires. Thirty-one people lost their lives.

> "The sheer amount of fire on the landscape is surreal, and no one I have talked to can remember anything like it."[26]
>
> —Nick Nauslar, meteorologist

Soon other western states were affected as well. "Multiple fires made 20-mile runs in 24 hours over the last few days in California, Oregon, and Washington," Idaho-based meteorologist Nick Nauslar reported in early September. "Most of these fires are making massive runs in timber and burning tens of thousands of acres and in some cases 100,000 acres in one day. The sheer amount of fire on the landscape is surreal, and no one I have talked to can remember anything like it."[26]

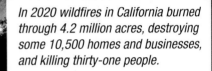

In 2020 wildfires in California burned through 4.2 million acres, destroying some 10,500 homes and businesses, and killing thirty-one people.

Among the people left homeless by the wildfires were Jill Rouse and her three children. The family moved to a cabin in rural Berry Creek, California, in 2018 after losing their home in a wildfire in nearby Paradise, California. In September 2020 a wildfire swept through Berry Creek as well, forcing Rouse and her children to flee the area. When they returned, the family discovered their new home had been lost in the fire. "This is literally identical to what happened last time," Rouse said. "It feels made up—like how could this even be happening to someone twice."[27]

By the end of the year, officials calculated that more than fifty-two thousand wildfires had spread across 8.8 million acres (3.6 million ha) in 2020. States that were affected included California, Colorado, Idaho, Oregon, Utah, Washington, and Wyoming. Experts warned that unless the effects of climate change are reversed, citizens of Australia, the western states of America, and other dry regions could expect similar degrees of devastation in the coming years. As for that 130°F (54.4°C) temperature recorded in Death Valley, Cristi Proistosescu, an atmospheric scientist at the University of Illinois, says, "Don't think of it as the warmest month of August in California in the last century. Think of it as one of the coolest months of August in California in the next century."[28]

Named Storms Hit the East Coast

Just as wildfires burned through thousands of acres in the western states, residents of the East Coast and other parts of America were experiencing very different effects of climate change. A series of devastating hurricanes and other severe storms swept through many states in 2020. Residents were often forced to evacuate to escape destructive winds or rising river levels that left many of their communities underwater.

Scientists believe climate change is a contributing factor to the creation of severe storms. As the earth's atmosphere warms, so do the temperatures of the world's oceans. Warmer ocean water tends to send more moisture into the atmosphere. Therefore, a relatively minor storm fed by excess moisture from a warm ocean can often turn into a hurricane.

The states along the Atlantic and Gulf coasts face hurricane season every year—typically from June 1 through November 30. In a typical year, a dozen named storms form in the Atlantic Ocean, some of which do find their way to the East Coast. In early April scientists predicted that due to the warmth of the Atlantic Ocean, as many as eighteen named storms could be expected to form in 2020. The prediction turned out to be low. Tropical Storm Arthur arrived in mid-May 2020, two weeks before the start of hurricane season. By the end of the year, thirty named storms had hit the country. In fact, there were so many named storms in 2020 that meteorologists exhausted all the letters of the alphabet. (Storms are typically named in alphabetical order.) To remedy this

Derechos Pummel the Midwest

Among the storms that swept through America in 2020 were several derechos—weather events that typically hit states in the Midwest. In Spanish the word *derecho* means "straight ahead," which characterizes the wind gusts found in the storms. Unlike hurricanes, which feature winds that swirl around a central "eye," winds from a derecho plow straight ahead, often leveling whatever is in their path. It is not unusual for a derecho to extend for hundreds of miles before its winds die down. According to meteorologists, derechos are fed by cool downdrafts of air that originate high in the atmosphere. As those downdrafts meet winds closer to the earth's surface, they form the powerful derechos.

The most devastating derecho of 2020 hit portions of Illinois, Indiana, Iowa, Michigan, Nebraska, Ohio, South Dakota, and Wisconsin on August 20. Among the hardest-hit cities was Cedar Rapids, Iowa, where hundreds of homes, schools, and businesses suffered damage. "Nearly every home has damage," said Cedar Rapids resident Ben Kaplan. "Most big trees in the city fell. Most local businesses are closed. Every business is damaged. Most roads are impassable."

Quoted in Sukee Bennett, "Inside the Derecho That Pummeled the Midwest," PBS, August 21, 2020. www .pbs.org.

problem, they resorted to labeling the final few storms of the year with letters from the Greek alphabet.

Hurricane Laura Levels a City

The most devastating storm of 2020 was Hurricane Laura, which formed over the ocean in mid-August, making landfall in southwestern Louisiana on August 27. Some 1.5 million people living near the Louisiana coastline were evacuated days before the storm hit. The community hit hardest by the storm was the city of Lake Charles, which has a population of about seventy-eight thousand people. Large portions of the city were leveled by Hurricane Laura and its wind gusts of more than 120 miles per hour (193 kph). Among the evacuees of Lake Charles were Rebekah Winstead, her husband, and their three-year-old son. Leaving Lake Charles before the storm hit, the family drove for ten hours to stay with relatives in Atlanta, Georgia. A few days later, the Winsteads watched TV coverage of the storm as it barreled through Lake Charles.

Days later, the family returned to Lake Charles to find their home destroyed. "We lost most of our things, the windows were smashed," Winstead says. "It's not livable, which is devastating. My son keeps asking to go home but we can't. It's heartbreaking to see your town completely demolished. . . . I never thought at 27 I'd be married with a three-year-old and homeless. But there are a lot of people in our position."[29]

For the families of Lake Charles, though, things would get worse. Before the hurricane season of 2020 ended, their city was hit by a second devastating storm. Six weeks after the city was hit by Hurricane Laura, Hurricane Delta swept through the region. Many of the homes or businesses that escaped destruction by Hurricane Laura were now hit with a second blast. As Hurricane Delta swept through town, Lake Charles resident Priscilla Sam found herself faced with the prospect of rebuilding the beauty salon she owns. In fact, after losing her home in the first storm, Sam moved into the salon, sleeping on an air mattress in a back room.

Hurricane Laura made landfall in southwest Louisiana in August of 2020, causing widespread destruction from high winds and flooding.

But Hurricane Delta damaged the roof of the salon and soaked the interior walls, damaging much of the styling equipment and supplies inside. "Everything I know is here,"[30] she said as she surveyed the damage.

By the end of the year, the weather forecasting service AccuWeather estimated property damage in America caused by the 2020 storms at more than $60 billion. In addition, the deaths of 144 Americans have been attributed to the storms by the National Oceanic and Atmospheric Administration (NOAA), a federal agency. According to NOAA, Hurricane Laura was responsible for 42 of those deaths.

For years, Americans and residents of other countries have endured storms and wildfires. But the intensity with which they arrived in 2020 was unprecedented. Scientists largely agree that the storms and fires were caused by climate change. They also warn that extreme weather is likely to continue until and unless the nations of the world decide to take concrete steps to slow climate change.

CHAPTER FIVE

The 2020 Campaign for the Presidency

In America the campaigns for president typically start long before the first votes are cast. Candidates start ramping up their campaigns a year or more in advance. They raise money, hire key campaign staff members, commission polls to gauge their popularity among the voters, and start touring the country, speaking at events to get their names mentioned in the media.

That is how the 2020 campaign for president commenced. By the summer of 2019, there were already a dozen Democratic candidates crisscrossing the country, lining up support for their campaigns. Meanwhile, on the Republican side, President Donald Trump prepared for a virtually uncontested path toward renomination by his party. Even so, he still campaigned hard, visiting dozens of cities throughout 2019. At the same time, his campaign committee raised millions of dollars for the extensive TV advertising and other expenses that are part of a national campaign for the presidency.

And so by early January it appeared the 2020 race for president would resemble past presidential campaign years. But this was, after all, 2020. As the campaign headed into the new year, Trump found himself facing an impeachment trial in the Senate. A pandemic soon started sweeping across the country. The attention of voters was often diverted by continued reports of police killings of unarmed Black Americans and the protests that followed. Said Charles Gerow, a Pennsylvania political consultant:

We are a nation as deeply divided as at any point since the Civil War. We've been plagued by the COVID-19 pandemic, and now face the daunting task of rebuilding an economy and social structures torn apart by the lockdowns and shutdowns of the past few months. In the midst of this we're now experiencing rioting and looting in most of our cities. . . . It's going to be an election like none in our memory.[31]

Trump Plagued by Low Poll Numbers

The incident that led to Trump's impeachment—the phone call to Ukrainian president Volodymyr Zelensky seeking to undermine the candidacy of Joe Biden—was prompted by the dismal poll numbers Trump saw in the summer of 2019. There were plenty of reasons for his low rankings in the polls. Voters found him brash. Rather than seeking common ground with his opponents, Trump instead resorted to ridiculing anybody who opposed his policies. He mocked

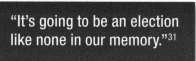

"It's going to be an election like none in our memory."[31]

—Charles Gerow, Pennsylvania political consultant

adversaries with crude nicknames. For example, he called Biden "Sleepy Joe"—clearly an insulting reference to Biden's age: the Democrat celebrated his seventy-seventh birthday in November 2019. (Trump was, however, not much younger—he turned seventy-four in June 2020.)

Trump's position on immigration was opposed by many voters. In 2018 Trump's "zero-tolerance" policy toward illegal immigration was revealed to include the separation of children from families who were seeking asylum. Hundreds of children were taken from their parents and often held in detention while their parents were deported back to their home countries. Many voters were also angry with Trump for his support of a cadre of racist White Americans who gathered in Charlottesville, Virginia, in 2017 for a rally. During the rally, one of the participants drove his car into a crowd of counterprotesters, killing a woman. When reporters questioned Trump about the events at the rally, the president

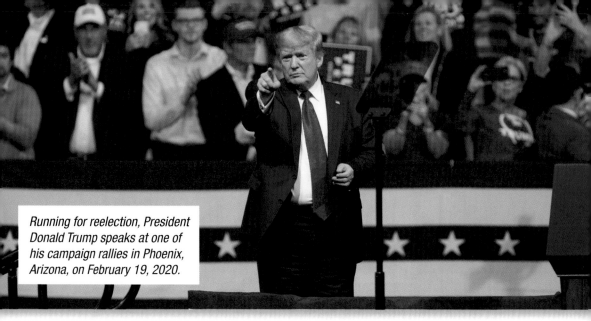

Running for reelection, President Donald Trump speaks at one of his campaign rallies in Phoenix, Arizona, on February 19, 2020.

said there was no place for violence at what should have been a peaceful demonstration—but he refused to condemn the racists who participated in the event. "You had some very bad people in that group," he said. "You also had some very fine people on both sides."[32]

Moreover, Trump completely dismissed the warnings of scientists over the dangers of climate change. A 2019 poll by the Washington, DC–based Pew Research Center found that 67 percent of Americans believed the federal government was doing too little to address the dangers of climate change. In fact, dating back to his first campaign for the presidency in 2015, Trump pledged to revive the coal mining industry in America, which had fallen on hard times as consumers and industries turned to renewable energy, such as solar and wind, and other resources to generate electricity. "We're going to get those miners back to work,"[33] Trump declared.

And by 2019 many Americans had lost their lives in mass shooting incidents, leading to demands by many citizens to enact new gun control laws. Trump vigorously resisted such demands—another factor in his poor standing in the presidential preference polls.

As Trump endured low poll numbers in 2019, Democratic candidates started lining up to oppose him. His impeachment and the Senate trial that followed seemed to further erode his support. By the time voters started casting ballots in the first caucuses and primaries in February 2020, a half dozen of the Democratic candidates were recording higher poll numbers than Trump. On February 10, 2020, a Quinnipiac University poll reported, "President Trump's favorability rating is underwater, as 42 percent of registered voters have a favorable opinion of him, while 55 percent have an unfavorable view of him."[34]

Trump Contracts COVID-19

As the primaries moved into March, the Democratic field started shrinking as candidates started dropping out of the running. By then, also, the breadth of the COVID-19 pandemic was becoming clear. In-person campaigning soon ground to a halt as most large rallies and similar events were canceled. Candidates were forced instead to appeal to voters through videoconferencing. And people soon found ways to cast their ballots other than through the traditional method of showing up at the polls. Many states loosened their rules for so-called absentee ballots, enabling voters to make their selections using mail-in ballots.

> "President Trump's favorability rating is underwater, as 42 percent of registered voters have a favorable opinion of him, while 55 percent have an unfavorable view of him."[34]
>
> —Quinnipiac University, poll from February 10, 2020

On March 17 Biden emerged as his party's front-runner when he won primaries in three states—Arizona, Florida, and Illinois. Finally, in early June he had the nomination wrapped up, winning enough delegates to guarantee his nomination at that summer's national convention, which ultimately was held online due to COVID-19 restrictions.

Meanwhile, voters found new reasons to question Trump's leadership. Early in the pandemic he made it clear that he disagreed with the directives issued by public health officials. His campaign continued to schedule rallies attended by supporters who often showed up without masks, huddling together in crowded arenas. As death tolls rose, he insisted the pandemic would go

Kamala Harris Makes History

Senator Kamala Harris of California made history in 2020 when she was elected vice president, becoming the first woman to hold that post in the nation's history. In previous years women had run for vice president as major party candidates— Democrat Geraldine Ferraro in 1984 and Republican Sarah Palin in 2008—but both candidates fell short of winning the post. Moreover, in 2016 Democrat Hillary Clinton lost the presidential race to Republican Donald Trump.

Moreover, Harris is multiracial—her father is Black and from Jamaica and her mother is a native of India. In addition to becoming America's first woman vice president, Harris is the nation's first Black vice president and the first vice president of South Asian descent. She is also the first vice president born to two immigrants in the nation's more than 240-year history.

Before serving in the Senate, Harris was California's attorney general. In selecting Harris to be his running mate in 2020, Democratic presidential candidate Joe Biden said, "Kamala knows how to govern. She knows how to make the hard calls. She is ready to do this job on day one."

Quoted in Savannah Walsh, "What Joe Biden and Kamala Harris Said During Their First Joint Appearance as Running Mates," *Elle*, August 12, 2020. www.elle.com.

away on its own. His administration was found to be doing little to help the states deal with the increasing numbers of victims—for example, refusing to provide masks and other personal protective equipment that health care workers needed to treat patients. And he refused to wear a mask himself. "It's voluntary," Trump said of the need to wear a mask in public. "You don't have to do it. . . . I don't think I'm going to be doing it."[35]

On September 26 Trump scheduled a ceremony in the Rose Garden of the White House to announce his selection of Judge Amy Coney Barrett for a vacancy on the US Supreme Court. More than two hundred people attended the event; most of them, including Trump, did not wear masks. Six days later, the White House disclosed that Trump, as well as several other people who attended the Rose Garden ceremony, tested positive for COVID-19. Trump spent three days in the hospital, ultimately surviving the ordeal. When he emerged from the hospital, he went back to speaking at campaign events where masks were largely not worn and social distancing was not practiced. "Don't be afraid of COVID," he declared after leaving the hospital. "Don't let it dominate your life."[36]

The Trump-Biden Debate

As Trump continued to appear at public rallies, Biden mostly remained home in Delaware, preferring to speak to his supporters through videoconferencing. He rarely ventured to other states, and when he did, crowds were held to a minimum and everybody wore masks. Finally, though, on September 29 Trump and Biden met onstage in Cleveland, Ohio, for a nationally televised debate.

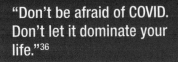

"Don't be afraid of COVID. Don't let it dominate your life."[36]

—Donald Trump, forty-fifth US president

Soon the event descended into attacks and name-calling, with Trump often interrupting Biden as he attempted to address issues raised by the debate moderators. Finally, an exasperated Biden turned to Trump and said, "Will you shut up, man? It's hard to get any word in with this clown."[37]

As Election Day neared, Trump raised a new issue that many political analysts, party leaders on both sides, and voters found shocking. The president strongly suggested that a conspiracy was afoot to steal the election from him. He blamed the preponderance of mail-in ballots that were sure to come as many voters elected to stay home due to pandemic concerns. And while he refused to provide details of how this alleged conspiracy was being carried out, he continued to issue dire warnings that the results of the November election should not be accepted.

Biden Declared President-Elect

On Election Day, November 3, millions of people showed up at their polling places to cast their ballots in person. But by then millions more had mailed their ballots to county election offices. Ordinarily, political analysts for TV networks are able to call the winners of presidential elections within hours after the polls close.

The analysts assess the unofficial counts coming out of the states as well as statistics generated by exit polling—wherein pollsters ask voters coming out of the polling places whom they selected in the presidential contest. But in the 2020 election, with so many mail-in ballots still arriving at election offices across the country, the TV analysts were unable to make those calls on election night.

Not until November 7—four days after the polls closed—were analysts able to call the election, declaring Biden the winner. During his victory speech that night, Biden declared his intention to unite Americans after what had been a very troubling year. "It's time to put away the harsh rhetoric, to lower the temperature, to see each other again, to listen to each other again, to make progress, we must stop treating our opponents as our enemy. We are not enemies," Biden said. "We are Americans."[38]

President-elect Joe Biden, accompanied by his running mate, Kamala Harris, delivered his victory speech on November 7, 2020. Addressing the nation, Biden promised to unite Americans after what had been a very troubling year.

Why the Mail Was So Slow

In addition to a pandemic, out-of-control wildfires, and a divisive presidential campaign, Americans found themselves enduring the fact that in 2020 the mail never seemed to arrive on time. Elaine Caruso of Allentown, Pennsylvania, says it took two weeks for a package to arrive from her granddaughter, who lives in nearby New Jersey. "This has been going on the last three months," Caruso said in August 2020.

Many Democratic leaders in Congress blamed Donald Trump for the slow-down, alleging that he ordered the US Postal Service—a federal agency—to delay deliveries so that millions of mail-in ballots cast in the November 2020 election would never be counted. Trump feared most supporters of his opponent, Joe Biden, would vote through mail-in ballots rather than risk exposure to COVID-19 by showing up at the polls.

In fact, in an August 2020 interview with the Fox Business Network, Trump acknowledged paring the budget of the Postal Service specifically to slow the delivery of mail-in ballots. "That means they can't have universal mail-in voting," he said. "They just can't have it." Despite Trump's attempts to slow deliveries, the Postal Service still managed to deliver more than 135 million mail-in ballots that were counted in the 2020 presidential election.

Quoted in Peter Hall, "Does the Mail Seem Slow? You're Not Imagining It," *Allentown (PA) Morning Call*, August 1, 2020. www.mcall.com.

Quoted in Deb Riechmann and Anthony Izaguirre, "Trump Admits He's Blocking Postal Cash to Stop Mail-In Votes," Associated Press, August 13, 2020. https://apnews.com.

But Trump would have none of it. He refused to concede the election—even after election officials in each state declared the results valid and final. His campaign organization challenged the results in many states in court, often alleging his unfounded theory that the election was somehow stolen from him. In every case, though, judges dismissed his challenges, clearing the way for Biden to be sworn in as president on January 20, 2021.

But even then, with so many court decisions going against him, Trump steadfastly refused to accept the outcome of the election. And he soon set in motion a series of events that would lead to chaos in Washington, DC, as hundreds of his supporters laid siege to the US Capitol, resulting in his second impeachment by Congress.

Assault on the Capitol

Members of Congress huddled under their desks. A violent mob had broken into the US Capitol building in Washington, DC. Armed activists roamed the halls, some trying to burst through the door of the House chamber. "This was the moment I thought everything was over," says Representative Alexandria Ocasio-Cortez of New York City. "I mean, I thought I was going to die."[39]

On January 6, 2021, hundreds of angry demonstrators broke into the Capitol. They burst through doors and windows, easily overpowering a small staff of Capitol police officers. They roamed the halls, vandalized offices, and stole records and laptop computers. Security cameras later showed members of the House and Senate being shepherded out of the Capitol through back doors by police officers, some within a few feet of where armed and marauding demonstrators dashed through the building.

The siege of the Capitol occurred as the Senate was preparing to take up what is otherwise a ceremonial task—the official certification of the 2020 presidential election results. In the weeks following the election, as President Trump steadfastly refused to accept the results, his strategy to prevent President-elect Biden from taking office focused on the certification vote. He called on Vice President Mike Pence to use his authority as the presiding officer over the Senate to cancel the certification vote—an act Pence refused to do. (And in fact, under the terms of the Constitution, cancellation of the certification vote was an act Pence was powerless to order.)

Finally, on the morning of January 6, Trump spoke at a rally of his supporters at the Ellipse, a public square a short distance from the White House. Members of the crowd were angry. They had earnestly believed Trump's rhetoric over the past several weeks claiming the election had been stolen from him. During his speech, he urged his supporters to march to the Capitol and demand that the certification vote be canceled. "We fight like hell. And if you don't fight like hell, you're not going to have a country anymore,"[40] he said.

The Second Impeachment

The demonstrators left the Ellipse and marched the few blocks to the Capitol. Instead of remaining outside and exercising their legal right to protest, the mob soon erupted in anger. Their siege was recorded by news cameras as well as cell phone video. For hours, they ransacked the building. Many shouted plans to murder Pence, House Speaker Nancy Pelosi, and other officials. Finally, reinforcements from the National Guard as well as the Washington, DC, police department arrived to quell the riot and make arrests. Dozens of people were injured, and five people died. Four of the rioters died in the melee—one by suffering a heart attack, another by suffering a stroke. One of the rioters, Ashli Babbitt of San Diego, California, was fatally shot as a police officer fired his gun into a throng of rioters attempting to break through a door. Another rioter, Rosanne Boyland of Kennesaw, Georgia, died after being crushed in a throng of demonstrators. The fifth person who lost his life was Brian Sicknick, a Capitol police officer who was struck on the head with a fire extinguisher as he tried to prevent rioters from entering the building. By early February more than two hundred rioters had been arrested for their parts in the siege.

Also facing justice was Trump, who was alleged by House members to have incited the riot through his incendiary language

On January 6, 2021, as the US Senate convened to officially certify the results of the presidential election, a throng of pro-Trump demonstrators stormed the Capitol. President Trump's incitement of the mob violence served as the basis of his second impeachment.

in the weeks leading up to the siege, including the remarks he made that morning in his speech at the Ellipse. On January 13 the House voted to impeach Trump a second time by a vote of 232 to 197. Unlike the first impeachment in late 2019, this time ten Republicans joined the Democrats in voting to impeach the president. The trial commenced in the Senate on February 9. Since Trump had already left office—Biden was inaugurated on January 20—a conviction in the Senate would not result in the removal of Trump from office but rather would bar Trump from ever seeking the presidency again.

The House managers presented their case to the Senate, showing videos of the assault as well as numerous film clips of Trump urging his followers to march to the Capitol and force Pence to dismiss the results of the election. Many senators said they were shocked by the security footage, realizing as they saw the film how close they were to being assaulted by the rioters. "[It] tears at your heart and brings tears to your eyes," says Senator Mitt Romney. "That was overwhelmingly distressing and emotional."[41]

Unlike the first impeachment trial in 2020, this time seven Republicans, including Romney, voted to convict the former president. All Democrats voted for conviction as well. The final vote was 57–43 in favor of conviction. Although a majority of senators now favored conviction, the final total still fell short of the two-thirds majority needed to bar Trump from seeking the presidency again. Trump remains free to campaign for the presidency again in 2024. And if he does seek a new term as president, the campaign will surely test the will of Americans who may find themselves as divided in 2024 as they were in 2020.

SOURCE NOTES

Introduction: A Year like No Other

1. Quoted in Mary Schmich, "Is 2020 Truly the Worst Year Ever?," *Chicago Tribune*, August 18, 2020. www.startribune.com.
2. Stephanie Zacharek, "2020 Tested Us Beyond Measure. Where Do We Go from Here?," *Time*, December 5, 2020. https://time.com.
3. Zacharek, "2020 Tested Us Beyond Measure. Where Do We Go from Here?"

Chapter One: The Impeachment of President Trump

4. Quoted in *New York Times*, "Read Alexander Vindman's Prepared Opening Statement from the Impeachment Hearing," November 19, 2019. www.nytimes.com.
5. Quoted in Politico, "Read Adam Schiff's Opening Argument at Senate Impeachment Trial," January 22, 2020. www.politico.com.
6. Quoted in Veronica Stracqualursi, "'I'm Not Trying to Pretend to be a Fair Juror Here': Graham Predicts Trump Impeachment Will 'Die Quickly' in Senate," CNN, December 14, 2019. www.cnn.com.
7. Quoted in Ian Millhiser, "Mitt Romney Just Did Something That Literally No Senator Has Ever Done Before," February 5, 2020. www.vox.com.
8. Quoted in Debbi Lord, "Trump Acquitted: Senate Votes 'Not Guilty' on Impeachment Articles, Trump Responds," Fox 13, February 6, 2020. www.fox13memphis.com.

Chapter Two: The Pandemic

9. Quoted in Caroline Radnofsky, "60 Lives 60 Days: Stories of Victims We've Lost from COVID-19 Two Months Since the First U.S. Death," NBC News, April 29, 2020. www.nbcnews.com/news.

10. Quoted in Agence France-Presse, "COVID-19, Pandemic and Lockdown: How 2020 Changed the World," Inquirer.net, December 27, 2020. https://newsinfo.inquirer.net.
11. Quoted in Alana Semuels, "No Income. Major Medical Bills. What Life Is like for Millions of Americans Facing Financial Ruin Because of the Pandemic," *Time*, May 7, 2020. https://time.com.
12. Quoted in John Kapetaneas et al., "How FBI Says Michigan Governor Kidnapping Plot Went from Texts, Small Gatherings to Raid," ABC News, October 20, 2020. https://abcnews.go.com.
13. Quoted in Kapetaneas et al., "How FBI Says Michigan Governor Kidnapping Plot Went from Texts, Small Gatherings to Raid."
14. Quoted in Demetri Sevastopulo and Kadhim Shubber, "Trump Cheers as Anti-lockdown Protests Spread," *Financial Times* (London), April 19, 2020. www.ft.com.
15. Quoted in Dave Altimari and Jenna Carlesso, "'It's a Nightmare:' A Growing Number of Seniors Are Unable to Book Vaccine Appointments as Problems Mount," Connecticut Mirror, January 22, 2021. https://ctmirror.org.

Chapter Three: Rising Up Against Racial Injustice

16. Quoted in Omar Jimenez, "New Police Body Camera Footage Reveals George Floyd's Last Words Were 'I Can't Breathe,'" CNN, July 15, 2020. www.cnn.com.
17. Quoted in Amir Vera and Paul P. Murphy, "What Protesters Say Is Fueling Their Anger," CNN, May 30, 2020. www.cnn.com.
18. Quoted in Jeremy Gorner et al., "Mayor Imposes Curfew After Chaotic Scenes Unfold in Loop, Near North Side as Protesters Clash with Police During Demonstration over Death of George Floyd in Minneapolis," *Chicago Tribune*, May 31, 2020. www.chicagotribune.com.
19. Quoted in Dennis Wagner, "'Peaceful Protests Got Hijacked': Some Criminals Used George Floyd Protests as Cover for Looting, Police Say," *USA Today*, June 18, 2020. www.usatoday.com.
20. Quoted in Zachariah Hughes et al., "3 Police Officers Injured as George Floyd Protest Escalates in Philly; Kenney Implements Curfew," WHYY, May 30, 2020. https://whyy.org.
21. Quoted in N'dea Yancey-Bragg et al., "'Secret Police Force': Feds Reportedly Pull Portland Protesters into Unmarked Vehicles, Stirring Outrage," *USA Today*, July 17, 2020. www.usatoday.com.

22. Quoted in Yancey-Bragg et al., "'Secret Police Force.'"
23. Quoted in CBS 4 Denver, "'I'm Proud of the Demonstrations': Denver Mayor Michael Hancock Marches with Protesters Downtown," June 3, 2020. https://denver.cbslocal.com.

Chapter Four: The Fires and Storms of 2020

24. Quoted in Concepción de León and John Schwartz, "Death Valley Just Recorded the Hottest Temperature on Earth," *New York Times*, August 17, 2020. www.nytimes.com.
25. Quoted in de León and Schwartz, "Death Valley Just Recorded the Hottest Temperature on Earth."
26. Quoted in Matthew Cappucci and Jason Samenow, "From Ferocious Fires to a Historic Hurricane Season, 2020 Took Weather to New Extremes," *Washington Post*, December 29, 2020. www.washingtonpost.com.
27. Quoted in Lena Howland, "'I Guess We Have Bad Luck': Family Loses Home in North Complex Fire After Losing Home in Paradise," ABC 10, September 12, 2020. www.abc10.com.
28. Quoted in Oliver Milman, "America's Year of Fire and Tempests Means Climate Crisis Just Got Very Real," *The Guardian* (Manchester, UK), September 30, 2020. www.theguardian.com.
29. Quoted in Milman, "America's Year of Fire and Tempests Means Climate Crisis Just Got Very Real."
30. Quoted in Rick Rojas, "After 2 Hurricanes, Lake Charles Fears Its Cries for Help Have Gone Unheard," *New York Times*, October 20, 2020. www.nytimes.com.

Chapter Five: The 2020 Campaign for the Presidency

31. Charles Gerow, "In a Year like No Other, We'll Hold the Election of Our Lifetime," *The Hill* (Washington, DC), June 3, 2020. https://thehill.com.
32. Quoted in Meghan Keneally, "What to Know About the Violent Charlottesville Protests and Anniversary Rallies," ABC News, August 8, 2018. https://abcnews.go.com.
33. Quoted in David Koenig, "AP Fact Check: Trump's Vow to Create Appalachian Coal Jobs," Associated Press, May 5, 2016. https://apnews.com.

34. Quinnipiac University Poll, "Sanders Takes Top Spot in Dem Primary as Biden Falls, Quinnipiac University National Poll Finds; Bloomberg Rises in Primary, Runs Strong Against Trump," February 10, 2020. https://poll.qu.edu.

35. Quoted in Daniel Victor et al., "In His Own Words, Trump on the Coronavirus and Masks," *New York Times*, October 2, 2020. www.nytimes.com.

36. Quoted in Lawrence Wright, "The Plague Year," *New Yorker*, January 4–11, 2021, p. 54.

37. Quoted in Grace Segers et al., "First Debate Descends into Chaos as Trump and Biden Exchange Attacks," CBS News, September 30, 2020. www.cbsnews.com.

38. Quoted in Jonathan Lemire et al., "Biden Defeats Trump for White House, Says 'Time to Heal,'" Associated Press, November 7, 2020. https://apnews.com.

Epilogue: Assault on the Capitol

39. Quoted in Meredith Deliso, "'Traumatic Experience for All of Us': House Members Share Personal Stories About the Capitol Attack," ABC News, February 4, 2021. https://abcnews.go.com.

40. Quoted in Brian Naylor, "Read Trump's Jan. 6 Speech, a Key Part of Impeachment Trial," NPR, February 10, 2021. www.npr.org.

41. Quoted in Catherine Garcia, "Romney Says Footage Shown at Impeachment Trial Let Him Know How Close He Was to Danger," Yahoo! News, February 10, 2021. https://news.yahoo.com.

Books

Marcia S. Gresko, *COVID-19 and the Challenges of the New Normal*. San Diego, CA: ReferencePoint, 2021.

Heather Hansen, *Wildfire: On the Front Lines with Station 8*. Seattle, WA: Mountaineers, 2020.

Hal Marcovitz, *Racial Injustice: Rage, Protests, and Demands for Change*. San Diego, CA: ReferencePoint, 2021.

Jon Meacham, introduction to *The Impeachment Report: The House Intelligence Committee's Report on Its Investigation into Donald Trump and Ukraine*, by House Intelligence Committee. New York: Broadway, 2019.

Jon Meacham et al., *Impeachment: An American History*. New York: Modern Library, 2018.

Internet Sources

Charles Gerow, "In a Year like No Other, We'll Hold the Election of Our Lifetime," *The Hill* (Washington, DC), June 3, 2020. https://thehill.com.

Oliver Milman, "America's Year of Fire and Tempests Means Climate Crisis Just Got Very Real," *The Guardian* (Manchester, UK), September 30, 2020. www.theguardian.com.

Alana Semuels, "No Income. Major Medical Bills. What Life Is like for Millions of Americans Facing Financial Ruin Because of the Pandemic," *Time*, May 7, 2020. https://time.com.

Amir Vera and Paul P. Murphy, "What Protesters Say Is Fueling Their Anger," CNN, May 30, 2020. www.cnn.com.

Stephanie Zacharek, "2020 Tested Us Beyond Measure. Where Do We Go from Here?," *Time*, December 5, 2020. https://time.com.

Websites

Black Lives Matter
https://blacklivesmatter.com

This civil rights group helps coordinate protests and other measures to oppose racial inequality. The website includes information on measures the group believes are necessary to halt racial injustice. It also provides photos and timelines.

Human Rights Watch: Ukraine
www.hrw.org/europe/central-asia/ukraine#

This Human Rights Watch website provides an overview of the eastern European country's border clashes with Russia, its hostile neighbor. Visitors can see videos of the border clashes as well as protests against Russian aggression and find articles written by foreign policy experts on political developments in the country.

Impeachment Related Publications
https://www.govinfo.gov/collection/impeachment-related-publications

Govinfo is a service of the US Government Publishing Office. It provides free public access to official publications from all three branches of the federal government. This website has bills, rules, precedents, and other documents related to impeachment inquiries and proceedings. This includes the two Trump impeachments and select past impeachments.

Intergovernmental Panel on Climate Change
www.ipcc.ch

An agency of the United Nations, the Intergovernmental Panel on Climate Change reports on changes in the environment that are attributable to climate change. Among the reports available on the agency's website are studies on how a warming climate sparks wildfires and severe storms.

National Oceanic and Atmospheric Administration
www.noaa.gov

This federal agency monitors severe weather events, including named storms. By accessing the link for "Weather," visitors to the agency's website can find videos recorded by satellites of hurricanes that hit

America in 2020. The agency's link for "Climate" provides statistics and facts about how climate change is impacting the earth.

Quinnipiac University Poll
https://poll.qu.edu

The national public opinion poll provided by Quinnipiac University in Hamden, Connecticut, gauges public opinion on numerous issues, including the popularity of presidential candidates. Visitors to this website can find news releases reporting findings of recent polls. The "Tips for Reporting" tab explains how to interpret the numbers reported by pollsters.

World Health Organization
www.who.int

Visitors to the website maintained by the United Nations agency responsible for monitoring pandemics can find many resources on COVID-19, including the latest infection and death statistics, updates on development of new vaccines, and instructions on how people can best protect themselves against infection.